Silent Tears No More

Rhonda Brown-Tunstall

SILENT TEARS NO MORE
Copyright © 2019 by
Rhonda Brown-Tunstall.
All rights reserved. Printed in the United States of America. No part of this book may be used or reproduced in any manner whatsoever without written permission except in the case of brief quotations em-bodied in critical articles or reviews. This book is a work of non-fiction. The contents of this book is an autobiography of the author and in good faith, assumes responsibilty for the truth or accuracy of the events, people, or information presented.

For information and permission contact:
Author
Rhonda Brown-Tunstall
SilenTNM@gmail.com

Book and Cover design by Designer: Shaun Johnson: SPJ Graphics – spjgraphicdesign@gmail.com

Editor: Betty Spencer
bettyspencer1863@gmail.com

Photograher:
Wendell R. McMillan II,
wriiphotography.com, IG
wriiphotography, FB

ISBN: 978-1-7923-0831-4
First Edition: May 2019

Dedication

First, I dedicate this book to my Lord and Savior Jesus Christ, who without Him, I am nothing. He trusted me with this cross to carry and gave me the strength to tell my story.

Secondly, this book is dedicated to several extraordinary people in my life. Without these individuals, I wouldn't be where I am today. To my mom and dad (Deceased) who conceived me. Thank you for fighting to keep me, for I am who I am today, because of you.

To my King, my protector, my best friend and my TARZAN, my husband, Pastor James W. Tunstall, you always believed in me, provided, loved me and gave me the opportunity to dream and grow. I thank God He gave me you.

To my marvelous children, D'Andre, Destinee, De'Ja and James, I am so appreciative to God that he chose me to be your mother. It has truly been a blessing to be your mother and to watch you grow as awesome leaders, examples and givers in your prospective communities and churches.

Table of Contents

INTRODUCTION

CHAPTER 1:   THUMBING THROUGH   12

CHAPTER 2:   WELCOME HOME   19

CHAPTER 3:   THE RELEASE PARTY   41

CHAPTER 4:   CHANGE IS GONNA COME   48

CHAPTER 5:   TROUBLE DON'T LAST ALWAYS   52

CHAPTER 6:   IT TAKES TWO   71

CHAPTER 7:   SILENT TEARS NO MORE   80

CHAPTER 8:   KISS AND RIDE   90

CHAPTER 9:   MIRRIOR! MIRRIOR! ON THE WALL   94

CHAPTER 10:   DRESS UP!   110

ABOUT THE AUTHOR

ACKNOWLEDGEMENTS

Introduction

About eight years ago this book was placed in my heart. I never thought I would actually get to a place in my life to be courageous enough to actually begin to write what was in my heart.

Today, I can, and it has changed the course of my life. My hope is that this book will resonate deeply in the lives of those who read it and that your emotional wellbeing will be transformed through it.

Although we will journey into the depths of my past, you will realize the importance of having a relationship with Jesus Christ, your marriage, your family, your job, your friends and you will be illuminated.

The acknowledgement of my childhood pain and emotional abandonment was difficult. The painful experiences and conditions in my life caused me to want to bury my past. I realized that my pain could be used for good and that my past misery can be turned into useful ministry.

I am thankful to God for giving me the strength, tools, resources, family and friends to write this book. Through God's love and His mercy, He has shown me how to write from a place of BROKENNESS and today I'M BETTER NOT BITTER.

I am a survivor of childhood emotional abandonment and a traumatic painful past. As I share with you my story and some of the steps, I've taken on how to get pass my past.

One important key, that I have embraced is that of a role model. Unbeknownst to me my journey has caused me to become a role model to others including my family. As many of them have watched and traveled with me through my painful life. Through God's love, guidance, my resilience, steadfastness and total dependence on Him, my examples, good or bad was seen by them all.

Although, my past at times made me feel angry, bitter, and hopeless, it has empowered me to show others how to turn their pain into passion, positivity and purpose.

My pain was emotional and had a devastating impact on my life, but it has now brought clarity, understanding, development and positive change to my life and to those around me. Whether your pain is physical or emotional, it can be used for good, to make a positive impact on others. As the devastation of my past and the emotional fog becomes apparent in this story, it has become clear that this pain is a bonding agent in my relationships with God and my family. Now, through the pain, I had once suffered, I can now identify with others going through similar hurts and pains.

Finally, my heart is full of gratitude being able to empathize with others has helped me meet the needs of my family, friends, acquaintances and strangers. God gave me hope and the healing that I needed. It's my prayer that this book can be used for good in helping to propel you into your purpose while finding your voice.

If you are ready to make this journey? I invite you to continue reading.

Chapter One:
Thumbing Through

But when she could no longer hide him, she got a basket made of papyrus reeds and waterproofed it with tar and pitch. She put the baby in the basket and laid it among the reeds along the bank of the Nile River. NLT Exodus 2:3

Silent tears no more has become my existence. My journey began when I was a small baby placed in St, Anne's Infant Home. One would say, I was given away, although, I would say, that I was placed aside for my own protection. Back in the 1970's when I was in an Infant Home, the nuns were not allowed to bond with the babies, I thus began my journey thru life. As I begin to crawl through the painful memories of my past, I'm petrified. Being a baby surrounded by strangers who were responsible for my care and were supposed to nurture me somehow leaves me with a strong sense of emptiness. I'm left with so many questions. When I cried who cuddled me? When I smiled, who kissed me, just because? Who assured me I was loved and protected me when I was scared? I was told, I remained at the Infant Home until I was two years old. After leaving St. Anne's Infant Home, I was placed into Foster Care. My Foster Care parents were Clarence and Dorothy Lowe, whom I lived with until around the age six or seven. I was always told that I was a vibrant little girl with lots of personality. The foster home had other foster children in it along with their own biological children. My mom and dad were teenagers on a mission to get their baby back. During this time, in my young life, my thumb had become my pacifier. It was my best friend and my go to for comfort, whenever I got scared. When I would suck my thumb, I would get punished. Some punishments were very harsh. I can remember having my arm painfully pinned behind my back. It was at these times, I would cry uncontrollably, but somehow my thumb would end up right back in my mouth. My father's name was Ronald Louis Brown, whom I was named Rhonda Louise Brown, after him. I'm told that my dad was a tall, dark and handsome and that he would come and visit me when he could. Gratification came when it was stated that he said, I was his little girl. Unfortunately, my dad's life was cut short, he was murdered when I was only two years old. I had another sister that was nine months older than me. My parents were under age that's the reason my grandmother had to make a parental decision to have me protected by giving me away. Then another year later, my little brother was born, although, I remained in foster care. I can now say, I survived foster care. But the day came, when I was reunited back to my family, my mom, my brother and my sister. Remember, my accounts are based off suppressed memories, as I recall them, in my adulthood. I still have blanks some of which have never been filled in. As mentioned before, I don't remember my father. Even today, I wonder, what kind of man was he? Was he funny, corny or dull? Was he a good father? Blank, Blank, Blank! When growing up, having blanks unfilled in my life, I began to fill them in the best way I knew how. I painted a perfect picture of what a loving family was supposed to be in my mind which allowed me to survive. My father was a hero to me because it was communicated to me over the years, he was murdered. I filled in my own blanks. Still left with questions, I asked myself, when did we bond, Mom? You know that bond that exists between a mother and her child, that thing that securely fastens, joins and affixes your relationship with your child? I know in my heart you took the time to visit me often, you told me you did. . I totally understand you had two other babies to care for and you being a baby, a youngster yourself. I get it, but I too became a mom of a child at a young age. I had to fill in the blanks and revisit my past silently to understand that the physical and emotional affection a child receives can influence the path and journey that they choose to take in life. Why am I doing this? Let me fill in the blank for you. There is someone growing up with emotional baggage they cannot seem to get rid of. This baggage is so heavy, daunting, unbearable and paralyzing us silently.

Chapter Two: Welcome Home

As I share my story, my past, my pain, and my truth, it at times left me with some resentment. My sister was the quiet one, and she was a mommas' girl. She was always tattle telling on me and my brother. My brother though, he was my partner in crime. Whatever he could do, I could do better. I was your typical tomboy, climbing trees, playing football and chasing cats. Every now and then, an old sibling rivalry fight would occur, and I was going toe to toe with him. When my brother sneaked out the house, guess who would be right behind him? At some point, I was on the back of his bike when we were crossing a busy two-way highway when we were hit by a car. All I know is we got up off the street, grabbed that bike, ran into the house and kept it a secret between the two of us. Momma couldn't find out that we were out of the house when we were supposed to be in the house. My leg was bruised and scarred but it was our little secret. Those days were positively the best to me. My mom would always dress me and my sister alike, people often confusing us for twins. Even still back then, I found myself always trying to fit in. For some strange reason and feeling I can't describe, I felt like a stranger in my own home. I was the darkest complexion of all of us kids believe me, my sister and brother reminded me of that almost daily. They would tell me, I was adopted. Funny thing, I believed it! One of the worst things was that, I was a bed wetter. I wet the bed so much, my momma threatened to make me sleep in the bathtub. I received so many butt whooping's for wetting the bed. I tried hiding it but that was pretty much impossible when you shared a bed with your sister. I wasn't allowed to drink anything after about 6pm. But I would go into the bathroom and fill my hands up with water and sip to my heart was content. Despite the fact, my mom was a hardworking, single mother, striving to keep a roof over our heads, we were on the welfare system for a brief time.

Once my mom received the social security check from my deceased dad we were off the system. In spite of this, we were always kept clean, neat, and well dressed. Where ever we went, people complimented us on how well we were dressed. We never had our lights cut off, water cut off and we were never displaced. Some days, I would wait on my mom to get home from work after a long day and I would serve her. I just wanted her to know, I would do anything to make her load easier. As we were getting older my brother was beginning to go on a detour. I thought that my mother's heart was broken beyond repair. She would travel the streets at night looking all over for him.

Often, I would hear my mom crying in the middle of the night. My brothers' detour ended up landing him in prison. It broke my heart too that my little brother was gone and separated from me, he was only supposed to be my partner in crime. Eventually, at some point, my mom met a man who she later married. He was a good provider for our family, one would say. Although, he was in the home, but not really a full part of our home, to me. Remember, I had painted a picture early on as a young child of the perfect family. He was my mom's husband is what he was, and she was his wife with three children that weren't his. I never called him dad and that's because I was never was told, that I could. He did teach me how to drive and he helped me to get my learner's permit. As I reminiscence, there were no father daughter dances, no sitting on the porch with a shotgun to shoot would be boyfriends, no birds and the bees talks. He just wasn't, what I had pictured a daddy to be like. We had a nice home. It had four bedrooms and a den. Subsequently, I had my own room all to myself. Sadly though, I continued to wet the bed. I wrestled many years with the question, why did I wet the bed? Trust me, I did not want to wet the bed, but I could not seem to be able to stop. Embarrassed, I struggled daily with trying to hide my bed wetting from my mom, siblings and friends. Moreover, my room was painted a bright yellow and therefore, deemed my safety net and my haven. I spent a lot of my time in my room. I was left alone with my own thoughts and imagination. Now, let me say this, I was the *ATTITUDE* queen. You make me mad and I wouldn't talk to you for a day, week, month or even a year. Now, who was I really hurting, doing this? Without hesitation, it was me, whom I was hurting. I would cut you off like a faucet, but no pain could match the pain I had already endured, so I thought. Later, I tried out for the pom squad at my high school and I'll never forget, my number was the last one called. I was number five. The coach said, I had potential and she felt that I deserved a chance to be on her squad. The poms were the coolest, most popular high school squad to be a part of. Here this tall, black, skinny, teenager with low self-esteem made the team. You couldn't tell me nothing or at least, that's what I thought. I fought through each routine with thoughts of inadequacies, low self-esteem, flaws and weaknesses. I never felt like, I belonged on the pom squad, after all, it was all the girls who were prettier, smarter and more confident than me. Well, let me tell you this. When, I put on that uniform it was unexplainably, so totally rewarding for me. It transformed me completely, whenever I wore my uniform. Finally, I was now a part of something great, a family, a team. However, trust me when I tell you the moment, I took off my uniform and the routines ended, I was right back in the state of loneliness and despair, just like always. At this time, my life seems to have become a brutal cycle. I just couldn't figure out how to break that nasty emotion of just not feeling I'm fitting in. Then the day came, when I met a guy. I fell in love with him, my first boyfriend. Now, all my fears are diminishing. Already in my mind, I was going to marry him because he was the best thing that had ever happened to me. At least that's what I contemplated. My boyfriend was the finest, kindest, smartest and funniest boyfriend a girl could ever desire. We walked around school holding hands and sharing all our secrets with one another. We were the bomb couple. Now, I was still a virgin and I just knew he would be the one to have it. With full excitement, I told him I wanted him to have my virginity and him only because I was in love with him. Remember he was going to be my forever love and the one I would marry. Yes, we were going to marry and have the best life together. This is what I had pictured in my mind even as a young girl. We had planned it all out, on how it would all go down, for him to be my first sexual experience. We figured out a day to skip school. So now it finally happened. I was so fearful and oh my goodness, I was so scared. The pain, I experienced was unreal. Then, when it was over, I looked down and the sheets were bloodstained. No one told me this part. After it was over and done, it was not as I thought it would be. Immediately the ringing in my ears of my mom's voice saying to me time and time again that all boys ever would want from me was my goodies/cookies to get in my panties.

Naturally, I didn't believe her. My boyfriend told me he loved me, so this is what we were supposed to do, right? So as time went on, I was not prepared for what would come next. My boyfriend got another girl and he broke my heart like you would not believe. Now here we go again, more rejection another abandonment, and now back to my inadequacies of not fitting in. In my mind, all I saw, or thought was that she was prettier than me, so I thought that all the boys wanted her. I was totally devastated all over again. By now, I didn't ever want to go back to school, everyone knew and to me it was too embarrassing and shameful. He now had a new girl on his arm, what? I mean after all I had given him my virginity. After time, I eventually got over him. Then, I met the boy who would become my first child's father. He was cute and he had his own car and boy did he had some trickery words that soothed me. He would pick me up and I would let him fondle me and kiss me because he gave me all the attention I desired. Now this time I was in love for real, so I thought. On one particular day I had agreed to go with him to his house. As soon as we got inside of his house, he raised up my skirt, and began to touch me in ways that I had never felt before. Although the way he was making me feel was unimaginable, in my heart it felt wrong, but it was too late he had his way with me. From this encounter, I found out I was pregnant, and he stop talking to me all together. Again, another spiral of rejection and abandonment. Finding out, I was pregnant terrified me beyond my comprehension, I knew I had to tell my mom, but how? I struggled with shame and the feeling of defeat and revealed my dirty little sin in a written letter. Too ashamed to face her, recalling her warnings, I just had to reveal the awful act I had committed. She was deeply disappointed by me and I felt that this was the very thing that destroyed what little relationship we had. Feeling like I had betrayed her, what was I going to do now? My mom told me she didn't know what I was going to do with a baby and told me, I could not bring a baby in our home. Mind you, by this time my baby sister had been born. I was so in love with her. As she grew walking, talking and running the house. During this difficult time, she was ultimately the bundle of joy, I needed in my life. My pregnancy had me feeling lonely, perplexed, frightened and disturbed. Truly, it was another difficult time where aloneness and solitude seemed normal. Those in my immediate family kept trying to encourage me, telling me that my mom would change her mind, once the baby was born. I even entertained the idea of adoption. However, being young, petrified and troubled, recognizing, how it felt to be given away, cancelled that idea. We attempted to allow my baby's father's grandmother to take the baby once born, but she lived all the way in Delaware, so I was spooked out of that choice. Well, my mom never did change her mind. So now another emotional roller coaster ride. Wait! Wasn't this the very same position my mom was in? This can't be happening. Fearing that I would have no place to go a decision had to be made. It would be my cousins who had volunteered to care for my child for me, while in their words, this would allow me the chance for me to get my life in order. Finally, my joyful day arrived, and I delivered my son Ronald D'Andre Brown a beautiful baby boy weighing in at 8lbs and 10 ounces on August 6, 1989. Only to have him for three short days, my son was placed in one car with my cousins and I in another. Nothing could compare to the indescribable pain I felt when I had to let him go. This was something that belonged to me, everything had always been taken away from me. Just like my daddy, and like my boyfriend. Now, here I am again, empty with a sense of loneliness. I have now done what was done to me. I've now given away my son, just like my mom was forced to give me away. I hated the world and everyone in it. I was young, uneducated, desperate, determined and silent through all my pain and despair. Although, I had graduated high school and had dreams of going to college, I couldn't think of anything, but my son. My mom was determined that I would graduate college to become a journalist. At least, my son was able to go to family, my cousins who took great care of him. My son was not given away, as I always thought, but he was shared, at least this is how I enlightened myself daily. I would go visit my son, as often as I could. Never did a day pass, where I wasn't plotting in my head on how and when, I would get him back to raise, love and to care for. I was consumed with it day and night. Life is going along for me and I obtained my first job as a clerk typist in the federal government. With now having a stream of income of my own, I was eventually able to move out my mom's house, I'm about eighteen years old. Feeling somewhat accomplished, I was even more determined to get my son back. Still having many obstacles, I remained empty, not quite having found my place of belonging. During my pregnancy, I had begun to go to a local church, where I was introduced to the Lord and I gave my life to Jesus Christ. Finally, was beginning to see a ray of light and God began to open doors for me in so many ways. Sometimes, it was almost unbelievable that someone loved me so much and His name was Jesus. I didn't even grasp that He was there with me and loved me all the time. Where had he been all my life? Why did He allow me to experience such pain, agony, misery and defeat? God are you there? So, while attending church at Bethany Way of the Cross Church, I met a young man. Remember, when I said previously, that I had been told that my dad was tall, dark and handsome. Well, let me tell you, this guy fit that description fully, on every level and more. I first laid eyes on this handsome creature at a stage play, I was staring in. In one of the scenes, there was a disco ball, shining lights, smoke and music. I was portraying that of a night walker. I had on a mini skirt and high heel shoes. We locked eyes and I just knew he was the one. He captured my very being. I was smitten by him. He could glance at me and I was like a little girl crushing on her first love. Now, going to church had me wanting more and more. At the time, remember, in my eyes I'm rejected, a disappointment, broken, lonely, but, whenever in his presence, I felt special. It was not long before he and I began a courtship. I'm seeing more and more light in my dark world. Still, when I reflect, I am so forever thankful to my loving cousin, who allowed me to rent her basement. I'm just beginning to feel a sense of being on my own. With no intentions on going back, I'm now out of my mom's house. Then the day finally came, when I got my son back. When I think of all I had to endure, the struggles, the trials and tribulations I sustained, the very thought of getting him back stunned me. I did not want to let him out of my sight. He brought such an overwhelming joy to my unfulfilled life. The only thing I wanted was to spend every moment with him, to reconnect and redeem the time, I had lost. In my heart, I felt, I had to prove to him that I never wanted to leave him in the first place. This was very challenging for me. The guilt of having to share my child consumed me. For the first time in my life, I had someone who unconditionally loved me, just the way I was, just for me.

> *"The beauty of life is, while we cannot undo what is done, we can see it, understand it, learn from it and change so that every new moment is spent not in regret, guilt common fear or anger but in wisdom, understanding and love."*
> Jennifer Edwards

Chapter Three:
The Release Party!

If we confess our sins, he is faithful and just to forgive us (our) sins, to cleanse us from all unrighteousness. 1 John 1:9 KJV

While writing this book, I am absorbed with tears of sorrow. I began looking for excuses as to why I was feeling emotionally drained, confused, and exhausted. This must be PMS, right? Then it hit me, like a ton of bricks. I came to the realization, that I never cried through the pain of it all. I never dealt with the anguish, guilt and despair. I was at my job and I had to close my office door and just cry. I'm having an ugly cry day with all the bells and whistles. I am crying like never before, but this particular cry is deep and it's literally exhausting me. This one went way beneath the surface. Finally, coming to the first realization that this cry had to occur for me to begin to release, all that I had been holding onto in silence for so many years. At long last, I realized in my heart, that I never apologized to my son for having to share him with my cousins. I never addressed his issues, his hurt, and his pain. I felt like I had failed him as a mom. Sound familiar? One day he shared with me that he was molested as a child. Once again, I was not there for my son when he was suffering abuse at the hands of a family member. Imagine hearing that from your baby. I didn't even know how to respond. Feeling like, I had done to him what had been done to me, I still suffered in silence. After some time had passed and I got up enough courage and strength, I grabbed my phone and called him up and said, I must apologize to you, for never apologizing to you, for not being able to protect you. I told him that, I love him and that I always have loved him. Further, in our conversation, I expressed to him that I spent most of our time together attempting to make it up to him, I was buying his affection, covering up guilt and ignoring his pain, trying to cover up my own pain. I went deeper, letting him know that I know he suffered some things as a child he should never had to go through, but that mommy wished she was there to protect him. Regardless of the choices I made, regardless of what got me in the situation I was in, I wasn't there for my son when he needed me most. A lot of mistakes were made, due to the fact, I didn't know any better, but when you know better, you do better. I praise God for this release party now. Silent Tears No More! It has been a journey. But I finally learned that the first step was forgiving myself. It has been the key and catalyst to moving me pass my past. Now, that I have sincerely forgiven myself, the dream can be obtainable. I'm reminded of a song, by Motown legend (Diana Ross) entitled, "I'm Coming Out!"

It's my song today, I'm coming out! I want the world to know, I got to let it show! Come on won't you join me in this release party, I've had countless pity parties, but now my sorrows have become my victories.

"I'm Coming Out!"

Yours can too!

I want to share a letter my son D'Andre wrote to me. This, also became part of my release, and yes, the ugly cry happened, once again. I cried like a big ole baby, some more. I am so glad I didn't give up on my son, our relationship and our love.

Dear Mom:

My feelings have been misguided and I have made a lot of mistakes that I hope you can forgive me for. I accept your apology and never expected one from you, but it was genuine, heartfelt and it has helped me toward forgiving and moving on. We have never been as close as we are today. We have had our ups and downs, but I love you and always will.

Mom, I would die for you. I am so glad you are writing this book so our story can help someone else. One day, I hope to be courageous enough to share my story. You raised me the best way you knew how, and I am grateful. I would not be the man I am today without the love, support, knowledge and care you have given me over

the years. You are blessed mom; I call you Blessed Mom!

Love,

Your Son D'Andre

Chapter Four:
Change is Gonna Come!

While in an effort, to bond and mend my mother and I's relationship, I began the path to forgiveness. This is something that I've always dreamed of but did not know how to obtain. I always felt in my heart, that if, I could just hear the words ,"Rhonda, I'm sorry and would you forgive me?" My life would be forever changed and all that baggage I carried, along with the feelings of abandonment would just all dissipate. My mom would suddenly be the mom I dreamed of, the mom who wiped

> *Forgiveness is about empowering yourself, rather than empowering your past. T.D Jakes*

my tears when I cried, listened when I complained, fought when I could no longer fight, climb into the bed with me when I was scared, and made me feel I was number one. However, the opposite happened. Forgiving was harder than I thought I am the strong one and showing vulnerability was not an option in my life. I had to find a way to move on without showing others, I was weak, broken and overall an emotionally damaged individual. I continued to hold my mom hostage. I wanted justice, I needed revenge for all the hurt, I felt was inside me, and all the pain she caused me. I had to forgive to live again. I first had to lower my expectations in what I wanted from my mom. Then, I had to forgive Rhonda to love Rhonda.

> *Forgive yourself for your faults and your mistakes and move on. Les Brown*

Next, I had to free my mother from captivity in my heart. Once, I forgave my mom, I could understand the scriptures as they became clearer to me, *Psalm 139:14 (KJV) I will praise thee; for I am fearfully and wonderfully made: marvelous are thy works; and that my soul knoweth right well. Jeremiah 1:5 (KJV) Before I formed thee in the belly. I knew thee; and before thou cames forth out of the womb I sanctified thee, and I ordained thee a prophet onto the nations.*

Thank God our relationship has grown over the years, God is still working it out. I no longer hold my mom hostage; I know now she did the best she could do with the resources she had available, to her. I can only pray she forgives me for not being able to forgive her. I love my mom and I appreciate the women she is today. Forgiveness is a brave first step to healing.

> I believe forgiveness is the best form of love in any relationship. It takes a strong person to say they're sorry and an even stronger person to forgive.
>
> Yolanda Hadid

Chapter Five
Trouble Don't' Last Always

For his anger lasts only a moment, but his favor lasts a lifetime; weeping may stay for the night, but rejoicing comes in the morning. Psalm 30:5 KJV

As I continued to try to undoubtedly make sense of the confusion and demoralization, of my past, I carried on through life. While attending church and being fully committed to my faith, I fell in love with that tall, dark and handsome man, whose name is James W. Tunstall. After two years of courtship we were finally joined in holy matrimony, May 29, 1993. I could not believe it, a single mother bruised and broken, that this guy wanted to marry me. Remaining in transparency, I married James mostly to escape my pain. Our union was predicated on the sense of someone loving me, and biblical principles, that it was better to marry than to burn, 1 Cor 7:9. Keep in mind, we are church goers. Our wedding day ended up being one of the worst days of my life. My family did not support me, so, all bets were on, for how long we were going to stay married. Although, I never felt their validation anyway. We were given six months to last through conversations and rumors. It was our church family members who financially supported us as well as some friends and coworkers. Judy, Barbara, Salena,

Gloria, Nadene and Grace Godwin were vessels God used to make our day momentous. It always seemed like a nonphysical fight amongst family and friends but these few stood the test. Now, let me continue with my journey, as I'll fast forward. I'm married now to my prince, my knight in shining armor. My tall, dark and handsome man. Everything is now going to be happily ever after, right? Right after we wed, I received a promotion on my job, an Industrial Property Manager. Basically, it was my job to inventory and keep track of the government's equipment located on Job Corps sites. As I visited each site, I met other young people who had similar stories like mine. So, I was asked to share in small groups, having been a young struggling single mother, myself. I travelled as often as one week per month, all over the world. My husband and I were young and clueless about this thing called marriage. Through our faith we were determined to make an undeveloped marriage between two people work. It had not come easy. We were verbally destructive to one another and sometimes in one of my emotional fits, I'd throw a fist or two. My husband came from the hood, NE Washington, DC, where I was introduced to chicken wings and mambo sauce, a little side bar, they are the best. He was raised by a loving mother and an alcoholic father. He did not see affection, nor did he truly understand how to love a woman let alone a wife. We were two broken people trying to make a relationship whole. I still can't believe we married one another with all the emotional baggage and brokenness we both had. Keep in mind, I had a son already who was three when we married. My husband tried to be a father to him, but it was troublesome because he only saw his father as a provider not a loving father. Although, we strived daily to make the marriage work the best way we knew how, it was not enough and at times we didn't think we would make it. God in his infamous mercy still smiled upon us and gave us an angel in my Godmother, Grace Godwin. Her name was fitting to her overall persona. She was placed in my life for a time such as this. Grace taught me a lot of things like cleaning. shopping, parenting and work ethic, to name a few. This woman of God, the surrogate mother to me. She also taught me how to be a halfway decent wife to my husband. She took the time and had the patience to teach me things that I didn't otherwise know. Within our relationship, I found a mother's love and affection. Instinctively, I directed all my abandonment issues onto my godmother. One day, I saw that she was beginning to do for another young lady the things that she was doing for me and it tore me up so bad inside that I thought she was abandoning and rejecting me. I blew up emotionally and I began to rant and rave. I don't know where all these feelings came from, but I balled my fist up and tore up my apartment. I picked up everything she had ever given me, threw it in a bag and when she came to pick me up, I launched everything out in the middle of the street. I said the worse things to her. She never gave up on me though and continued to stay in my life. This behavior, naturally, would bring back all the times what people had declared over our union anyway, that it would not last. My husband could not fix me, nor could I fix him. For years, my husband was a safety net with a huge hole in the bottom. I know that because of my own emotional abandonment and emotional disconnect it was causing our marriage to suffer tremendously. We didn't understand each other, nor did we at the time, know how. Then, look what happens next. While James and I are were still learning how to be husband and wife and how to become a family it proved to become even more challenging when we discovered we were pregnant with our first-born. Our daughter Destinee was conceived. This delightful bouncing baby girl was born in 1995 and was the light in my seemingly dark tunnel. I would barely let her dad even hold her. I found that I would consistently cling on to her for dear life not wanting anyone to pull her away from me. Deeply seated within me, was all my emotional hurt and pain, which I believe caused me to over compensate my love for this child, while covering up my own insecurities as a mother. Her birth, somehow, God used to help grow James and me. We were now a loving husband and wife. At least on the surface, but we began to function and grow together. Hurt helping the hurting. Now, D'Andre, as he grew up and started grade school, he was diagnosed with ADHD (Attention Deficit Disorder). I was called to pick him up from school on countless occasions. D'Andre would crawl under desks and bark like a dog. He would get into fights with other students and even with teachers. D'Andre was placed on medication that made him like a zombie. Unfortunately, at the time, I had no clue, it was a controlling mechanism.

During this time, I didn't care, because I had a job and I couldn't keep taking off. By the time high school came he was put in a non-public school in Laurel and instead of things getting better they got worse. I remember my husband and me placing my son in a Christian summer camp when he was about ten years of age. One day the Director called us in for a conference and he explained to us that he had seen some signs of homosexuality in our son. Of course, I was furious and denied the accusations to the fullest. We brought him up in the church and this was an unspoken sin. What shame would this bring to my family? I could not and would not see such a sign, rebuking the thought in the name of Jesus. Subsequently, the day of reckoning came, that moment that destroyed my heart. I walked in on my son with another boy around his teenage years. As I looked at their naked bodies, I cringed in unbelief. You can't imagine the sorrow, guilt, shame, and familiar betrayal I felt. I reached out to the church and told my muddy little secret. My desire for an exorcism did not occur. Instead we were told to keep it secret. Again, the cycle continues. In return, my son never received therapy, help, support or love through this process. We went on as a polished, wholesome, good Christian family. I didn't realize, I was repeating family traditions and curses that could ultimately pulverize my family relationships. My family has held on to secrets for years. I no longer want these secrets to destroy my future, our future. So, because I was instructed by my family and my church family to keep hidden truths and to keep secrets, I've decided to expose the enemy right here and right now. Church, we must wake up! I Just want to communicate this because my son has chosen an alternative lifestyle and it's his choice. Guess what people? D'Andre is still my son, I still love him and most importantly, God loves him. Therefore, instead of us paying attention to what his alternative lifestyle is, just love him and pray for him, God will do the rest. I no longer need to roll the boat of guilt and shame. I no longer believe it is something that I did. What I want you to do for me, is to go, run and tell that. Continuing, with my story. Our family continued to grow. December 1997, our little Chunky, as we affectionately call her, was our third born. Her name is De'Ja. Having her was like De'Ja vu. De'Ja was quiet and always stayed under the radar. De'Ja reminded me of my older sister so much. This one right here, stole my heart and has kept running with it ever since. She and her little brother James stayed fighting from the day James was born. She never got in trouble and she was clearly the favorite with my mom and sister. My mom and sister would shower her with gifts. The very thing, I never experienced, I got joy out of my daughter receiving it. The cycle I said, I wouldn't allow, I was allowing it to run throughout my family tree. I think by the time I had De'Ja practicing was pretty much over and I was getting the hang of parenting. She is also my mini fashionista. De'Ja, a lot like me, we don't say a whole lot, but when she does everybody listens. De'Ja will be graduating college soon and I cherish our relationship. She is the comedian of the family. Then another gift from God. Our son James Jr., he was born October of 1999. James was a whopping 8lbs and 14 oz. He was the biggest of all our children. James our baby boy grew up also being diagnosed with ADHD (Attention Deficit Disorder). James had behavioral issues that kept my husband and me in the principal's office. He was constantly teased because of his size by other kids. He was placed on medication that made him a walking zombie. James was the poster child for Adderall, scoring the highest on test, becoming an A student and the teacher's pet. James began to play football. His size and heart couldn't be taught. He is working what God gave him. He attends the University of Connecticut where he is celebrated for what God has given him. For years, my husband and I allowed this to happen until we educated ourselves. We decided to take a stand and take James off medication and if that meant living at the school, oh well. Thank God for Jesus because once we abolished the medication, James started gaining healthy weight, he became a leader in the classroom, and he expressed his feelings. This was a remarkable milestone for my family.

> *"Small daily improvements over time lead to stunning results."*

This portion of my family's ups and downs is Important, because it's not how you start, but how you finish.

> *Wherefore seeing we also are compassed about with so great a cloud of witnesses, let us lay aside every weight, and the sin which doth so easily beset us, and let us run with patience the race that is set before us, Hebrews 12:1 KJV*

If you were to ask my children who the favorite is, I believe they will tell you "me". I know I wasn't the favorite growing up and it affected me even as an adult, but I had to try not to put the washing machine on repeat cycle when raising our children. I did not want my issues to fall upon them nor, for the cycle I spiraled through, to be repeated any longer. I had to come out and release and break the curse that kept me in silence, for so many years. Did I mention, I stop wetting the bed after the birth of D'Andre. As embarrassing as it was for me, it was not until then, that I finally stopped. Even today, I don't really know why I was a bed wetter, but I certainly believe that having gotten pregnant, God knew when it would cease. I'm free today and not ashamed to share my past hurts and blemishes. Today, I celebrate each of my children's accomplishments. Destinee is married she and her husband Mike have blessed us with our first grandchild (baby boy) Messiah, the newest apple of my eye. This child Destinee is the epitome of strength and determination. She often shares with me how she uses my past as an example in her classes as she is studying to be a Social Worker. Destinee says, because of my past and transparency her desire to be a social worker was formed. I can't believe my baby has had a baby and because the curse has been broken, our legacy can prosper. Destinee was our first-generation college bound, and the first to finish college in our family. Let me make mention of this. My husband James and I did survive marriage 101 and we are more in love today than the day we laid eyes on each other. God has been our sustainer. God had never given up on me.

Chapter Six:
It Takes 2

How could one chase a thousand, and two put ten thousand to flight.........Deuteronomy 32:30 KJV

One can chase a thousand. Strong relationships are imperative to your wellbeing. You must work on your relationships daily. If you are a mother hoping to renew, revive, develop a relationship with your child, I urge you start a project with your child. This project is one you and your child/children can work on together to strengthen your bond. My daughters and I decided we wanted to grow our legacy. We always knew we had an eye for fashion, so we sat down and developed a plan to establish our very own fashion boutique. The name It Takes 2 is essential to me. We are relational beings believing we were given two eyes, legs, arms, and hands to depend on one another. I must admit, that because I am being transparent, I want you to know, I vicariously have lived through both my daughters. I was guilty of overcompensating for my mother's emotional absenteeism. At times, I admit, I gave them too much of me that you could not see them. I found out quickly that it wasn't healthy for me to do so. I had to find a balance point to give them what they needed while encouraging them to learn and grow, as I am still doing so daily. I need my daughters to be whom God created them to be. People often ask us about our relationship as mother and daughter and how we are an excellent example to mothers and daughters. Today, Destinee, De'Ja and I have formed an unbreakable bond as mother and daughter. Even now, our close relationship is noticed by strangers. Mothers and daughters alike have witnessed our bond, whenever were out in public together. I always told my baby girls they are destined for greatness. I give God all the glory because He has guided me through each and every chapter of our relationship. I celebrate my girls. Here are some tips for you and your children that has benefited me. I believe you can use these tips to build upon:

- Don't ever stop loving them.
- Give up your right to be right.
- Always find time to laugh together.
- Make sure they know their point of view matters.
- PRAISE and AFFIRM them daily.
- Teach them to believe in themselves.
- Spend lots of time together.
- Start mother daughter/ mother son traditions.
- Focus on the positive aspects of your relationship.
- Often, write letters and notes to one another.
- Pray with and over one another.
- Always say I LOVE YOU!

Parents Are the ultimate role models for children. Every word, movement and action have an effect. No other person or outside force has a greater influence on a child then the parent." Bob Keeshan

Here is a letter my daughter De'Ja wrote to me:

Dear Mommy,

Back in February, I attended a Christian conference in North Carolina. While at this conference, we had prayer breaks. During prayer, I began to pray and thank God for so much. Then, when I began to thank God for my parents my face began to flush with tears. I truly thank God for you.

You always kept me happy, safe, protected and nourished. You are one of the most committed moms, I know. You attended every basketball game, cheerleading competition, awards ceremony, and anything else, that I was involved in. You never pushed me to be anyone I wasn't. I wasn't forced to do anything; I didn't want to do. You allowed me to be De'Ja. During my college journey, there has been many times when I called you while frantically crying on one end of the phone saying "Mommy, I want to come home." You gave me options, but never allowed me to give up. You've encountered more than your share of troubles and trials in life, and you've showed me what it means to not break under pressure, nor be so delicate that the storm washes you away. I have seen God strengthen you and build you up to be the strong woman you are today. I will never stop being fascinated that you have let these trials grow you into a pillar of faith. I am so proud of you for finally sharing your wonderful story. The words "I love you" are not sufficient enough to express how blessed I am to be your daughter; how much you are appreciated or how much you will always mean to me. I simply will say thank you for being my superhero.

Love,
Chunky (your um-um good Campbells chunky soup daughter)

This is why I live to be a parent. It is gratifying when as a parent that all you have sacrificed and invested in is striving to make the mark.

Please make it a point to provide a good example for them to follow, establish clear rules, to except responsibility, that their feelings matter, and that you love them for who they are.

****

****

****

****

****

Chapter Seven
Silent Tears No More

My Tears have been my meat day and night, while they continually say unto me, where is thy God? Psalm 42:3 KJV

My family and I enthusiastically joined a new ministry. Faith Assembly of Christ. I never felt so much love and what I perceived as acceptance. I recall upon arriving, I couldn't even cry. I had learned how to successfully bury my feelings; I didn't even know how to shed a tear. The thought of my past would instantly cause me to put a wall up to protect my feelings. I didn't even know, that I could cry, until I felt safe to discuss my past. My pastor Bishop Mitchell A. Way was so empathetic and sympathetic to the brokenness and pain I was carrying with me. He assembled the saints together and threw me my first birthday celebration. It was amazing, so very thoughtful and full of love. It was all about me and it felt so good but uneasy at the same time. I wasn't used to anything being about me or me being celebrated. Bishop was transparent and would always share his childhood hurts and pains as well. I sensed a place of safety and was slowly beginning to share my pain. As I began to discover new relationships and friendships, I was engaged in a conversation with Sister Jocelyn McClure and she assisted me in the process of learning to cry for the first time. She later became my Big Sister who would tell it to me straight even if I wanted to hear it or not. Every friendship needs a person like this. My other sister friend was Cynthia Summers. Her smile and her large family drew me closer to her. She has seven children and could cook Sara Lee out of her job. We developed a closeness in our families where our kids would refer to each of us as Aunt Rhonda or Aunt Cynthia. My kids loved going over her house to eat, laugh, and play, never being a dull moment at the summer's home. Our families enjoyed sharing holidays together and we shared some good times and bad times. This was a part of my life where I began to learn about true friendships and relationships. It was then I was beginning to learn deliverance from the spirit of rejection. It was a series Pastor Way taught; I couldn't fully grasp the concept of relationship totally. I have since asked my sister friend Cynthia for forgiveness because when you know better you do better. Because I was emotionally sick, I formed a codependent friendship with Cynthia not knowing at first that it was unhealthy. I thank God for placing her in my life don't get me wrong. She was strategically placed there for a time, a reason and a season. However, we as Christians sometimes will shout through the lesson we are to learn. Please understand that I do not want you repeating the same unhealthy relationship patterns despite your intentions just as I did. I was codependent on our friendship, making unrealistic demands on her time and trying to control her moods and actions. When I couldn't get her to focus solely on me and our relationship it would throw me into a depressive state. I hope I'm helping someone here. Because of my own dysfunctionality and childhood issues, I developed a codependency on people who paid me attention. It had become a coping mechanism that enabled me to suppress my feelings. I carried baggage of low self-worth and low self-esteem and that feeling of rejection. I used my friend to try and fix what was broken in me. Moving forward, I now totally depend on God!!!

Only God has the power to meet that need in us only, if we allow him. Silent Tears No More. I am no longer ashamed of my past. I am an Overcomer. I no longer place the blame of my past on others, because I choose to come out and celebrate, who I am today. Silent Tears No More, because I want the world to know that silently you die but openly, you'll thrive. You are never alone, I found out through my silence that God heard my whispers and was the real keeper of my soul. Find your voice even in silence and you'll hear another voice, if you yield to it and make the first step

> *Silent Tears No More, because I want the world to know that silently you die but openly, you'll thrive.*

in moving pass your pain into your purpose. Silent Tears No More. I am no longer bound but free to be me and share my experiences to set others free and who may have fell captive. Sometimes in life God will uproot and remove you out of that dry place that place where you're not receiving sunlight, the place that you're not being nourished or watered. I was in a dryland a sunken place. I'll tell you of a time that I know God connected me and directed my path. He connected me to a genuine family, Created to Empower Others and how they have rallied around me and my family and have shown me how to use the voice God has already given me that was muted for all of these years. They really introduced me to myself in many ways. A lot of times we spend years hiding our true selves or we become so busy trying to become what others think we should be we lose sight of who God wants us to be. I've learned through this organization my purpose, my purpose is to be a curse breaker, my purpose is to reveal secrets, and my purpose is to help someone else get to the roots that will allow you to examine yourself. I'm reminded of the scripture that says in Proverbs 3:6

> *When I get off the path my God has laid for me my life becomes challenging, but if I just stick with God, my path becomes clearer.*
> *Rhonda Brown-Tunstall*

(KJV), In all thy ways acknowledge him and he shall direct thy paths.

I thank God I allowed Him to direct my path.

If you don't get to the root of what's holding you back what's keeping you from growing and becoming great, you'll never see the manifestation of an abundant life.

> *"Learn to get in touch with the silence within yourself, and know that everything in life has purpose. There are no mistakes, no coincidences, all events are blessings given to us to learn. " Elizabeth Kubler-Ross*

Here are a few tips I used as God has begun to heal me, feel free to try these:

- See Yourself as Reliant, Smart, and Capable.
- Say goodbye to abusive behavior.
- Adopt a healthy outlook on what others say about you (good or bad) (your self-esteem should not determine what others think.
- Learn the word No and accept to hear the word No!

Chapter Eight
Kiss and Ride

All my life, I had been fighting this feeling of rejection and insecurity, the struggle of trying to fit in with others, the sense of personal advocacy and a sense of belonging. Someone once said, validation is for parking only. I say validation is real. The real truth is that without some kind of validations we allow ourselves to become an emotional mess. Like me this can become a daily battle that you fight and never win. So, how do I win a losing battle? I'm glad you asked! Because, you can never become validated when you are your worst enemy and over critical of yourself.

Try these steps on your path to winning:
- Start a personal journal
- Recognize and celebrate all the good things about you.
- When Seeking External Validation, whatever you want someone to say about you, Tell it to yourself first.
- Recognize Your Feelings, you have a right to feel the way you feel.
- Talk to Your Inner Child, let the inner child know that they are going to be safe and secure.
- Address Your Needs.
- Whatever you are feeling at the time, find out what's needed to feel better for example: Prayer, walking, talking to a

very close supportive friend or family member.

So, Let's Park and __Validate!

ALL WE NEED IS GOD'S VALIDATION TO FULLY SUCCEED.

I am ....

I am Loved!

I am Secure!

I am Enough!

I am who God says I am!

I am the Head and not the tail!

I am Fearless!

I am Confident!

Now You Write Some....

Chapter Nine
Mirror! Mirror! On the Wall

Today my reflection of myself is no longer distorted. Looking in the mirror and seeing me had been my daily struggle. I did not like or love myself. In my school age years, I would always wear flats because I was tall. Boy did I hate being tall. I was teased for being the tallest in my class. I didn't like my nose; it was too big. I didn't like the chicken pox mark left in the center of my forehead. My teeth were no help, they were crooked and uneven. Every time I looked in the mirror, my reflection was devastating, depleting, and degrading. Not only did I hate the person looking back at me, I hated the little girl inside. I was super critical of the little girl who always felt she wasn't enough. I was sabotaging the person I was to become, devouring the little girl inside, and wanting her gone by any means necessary. This little girl had to go, or at least that's what I believed and so the suicide attempt on my life failed. Every time I looked in the mirror, I would see the failed suicide attempt along with the shame and guilt. This brings me to this; we have all worn make-up or know someone who has. I'm not talking about that Mary Kay, Mac or maybe it's Maybelline! You see, the make-up I'm talking about is a make-up of a different kind. I'm not speaking of that contour look or beat face finish. You see, the make-up I'm referring to is the mask we wear. In my adult years, makeup became a mask. A mask, I wore every day. A mask I would hide all my insecurities behind; not just the blemishes, but hopelessness, rejection, suicidal tendencies, self-hate, bitterness, shame and guilt in silence. I never left home without it. I would try to compensate for the ugly within by covering up my face which the makeup helped me hide. It was what I put on every morning, to make it appear like, I had it all together. One day, I realized that if I wanted to shed myself of the insecurities and emotional feelings, I developed, I would need to start with the mask that was keeping it all in and hiding everything. It was time to wipe it all away.

Today, if you can relate to me and my story, I want you to get in the mirror and start wiping off:

- Childhood hurts
- Broken relationships
- Low self-esteem
- Sexual, physical and emotional abuse
- Generational curse
- Dysfunction
- Insecurity

I know it's hurtful and painful, but you must do this to discover that you love the face you see in the mirror every day. I was taught to fake it till I make it. I looked good; I was smiling but I was disintegrating and dying on the inside. BUT GOD!!!!! You can get rid of that polished image. You can STOP pretending.

> *"Wearing a mask wears you out. Faking it is fatiguing. The most exhausting activity is pretending to be what you know you aren't".*
> Rick Warren

I was tired, worn out and exhausted. Today, I want you to appreciate the artistry and self-expression of makeup as it was intended to be an art, and enhancement to our natural looks. I am in the fashion industry so make up is what helps my brand shine. If you know me, you know I love eye-popping glitter with every fiber of my being. I now understand makeup is not what makes me beautiful, it is I who make me beautiful. You are BEAUTIFUL and your past does not have to define you! God doesn't make junk and as far as I know, He doesn't issue recalls either! Finally, I concluded, it's not all about me and it never was about me, but it has been through me that I can let go of my past and be Silent No More.

> **It's not about make-up but about being made. I'm not talking about that Mary Kay, Mac or maybe it's Maybelline!**
> **Rhonda Brown-Tunstall**

Now, will you grab a mirror with me? Let's grab a mirror, now take a deep look into that mirror. Really look! Great! Now who do you see?

_____

_____

_____

What reflection do you see?

_____

_____

_____

_____

> *Keep Your Heels, Head & Standards High!*

I have an affirmation I do daily. Rhonda, Keep Your Heels, Head & Standards High! I accept my height, my nose, chicken pox and all. I am working what God gave me. We often complain about how we look. I used to tell a funny story when I met women. I would say I was standing in line up in heaven before my heavenly God as he was handing

> *Work What God Gave You!*

out booty's. When it was my turn, he said he was sold out. I THOUGHT THIS WAS FUNNY. However, if I had known back then, that I all I had to do was to accept what God had given me, I wouldn't have wasted all that time on what I didn't have. So, like a Porsche my junk is in the front and these cars are expensive and highly customized.

> *"I discovered who I was when I discovered God. You are just like your father God."*
> **Myles Munroe**

Steps to Getting Pass Your Past:

➢ Identify what (IT) is that has or is still hurting you.

_____

_____

_____

➢ Seek God, Pray, Fast and Read the Word of God.

_____

_____

_____

_____

- ➢ Face Feelings of Anger, Resentment and Hurt - Go to the root of your pain.

  _____

  _____

  _____

  _____

  _____

- ➢ Feel and accept what you are feeling deep down inside, your feelings and emotions matter but remember these emotions are based on past events.

  _____

  _____

  _____

___

___

___

➢ Name that feeling - Fill in the blank, I Feel:

___

___

___

___

➢ Forgive Yourself.

___

___

___

___

- Journal - journal your thoughts and feelings, this can help you navigate through your past without anyone judging or negating your feelings.

_____

_____

_____

_____

_____

_____

_____

_____

_____

_____

➢ Find an Empathetic Friend - find someone you can talk to about your experiences and your abandonment as a child.

_____

_____

If you are following these steps to recovery, you should be able to start moving away from your past (literally) it helped me immensely.

I encourage you now to follow these steps:

- ➤ Forgive the Person who hurt you - after examining the reasons my mom emotionally abandoned me, I had to accept it and forgive her for her shortcomings.

(Note: forgiveness does not change the past).

_____

_____

_____

_____

Change the way you think - ok it happened, you must accept it and move past the pain.

➢ Learn to Trust – I know it's difficult to trust again but it is key to your healthy being

_____

_____

Chapter Ten
Dress UP!

For I know the plans I have for you, declares the Lord, plans to prosper you and not to harm you, plans to give you hope and a future. NIV

Let's play a little game called dress up! How many of you have played dress up when you were kids? I remember all I ever wanted was to be like my mom. When she was a way at work, I would put on her high heel shoes look in the mirror and declare I was my mom. I wanted to be just like her. I was a child and I had fun playing that game. I didn't know at the time that I didn't need to be just like my mom or any other person for that matter, but whom God created me to be. So, over the years, I had to learn to dress up in a different kind a way. I had to dress up a better life for me. I encourage you to dress up your life today. However, you choose to use your past experiences to help others, draw a distinct line between THEN and NOW. Yes, it happened, and I wasn't treated the way I deserved to be treated and nurtured, but my past does not have to define my future. I don't look like what I've been through. As an emotionally abandoned child, I couldn't fight back, I had no power. But now that I'm an adult, I choose to focus on what I've learned through my experiences and not necessarily what has been taken away. Healing is power! My passion for fashion has propelled me into MY NEXT! Being married to my Tarzan, I had to dress up like Jane, and God has given me 25 years of an unbreakable bond with my husband. My future is hopeful not dreadful. Guess what? You can dress up today!

Remember:
- ❖ Focus on the outward (we dealt with the inward)
- ❖ Move toward Helping Others out of the fire
- ❖ Be everything YOU want to be

Congratulations! Just like I had the courage, you have the courage to face what has kept you from moving forward in your future. I applaud you! With this information, in this book, I hope that I may have helped you to overcome your past, not cry silently anymore and to take charge of your future.

Acknowledgments

I want to give all glory to God first and foremost. God has delivered me from my past and has done a mighty work in my life.

To my husband, Pastor James W. Tunstall, my Tarzan, my best friend, my ride or die, my security guard. God gave me a true man of God. My husband has been there for me in so many ways. Thank you for believing in me when I didn't believe in myself. For years you told me to write a book and to tell my story and I couldn't see it then, but you opened my eyes to my purpose, my promise and my passion. You patiently helped me unpack my emotional baggage throughout the years, not judging me or not killing my dream. I love you so much and we will do our next book on marriage together.

To my children: D'Andre, Destinee, De'Ja and James Jr. You all have given me so much. I have the best children on earth. You all have always supported me and given me the motivation to be the greatest mom I could be. Raising you all has given me the best gift of a mother I could have ever imagined. I am so proud of each of you and all your accomplishments and achievements. D'Andre is a manger of a large corporation. Destinee is married and has blessed me with my first grandson (Messiah A'King Savage) and is graduating from her master's degree in May 2019 in Social Work. De'Ja will be graduating with her undergraduate degree in Computer Information Science, May 2019. James Jr. is entering his junior year fall 2019 on a full D1 Athletic Scholarship. Eyes have not seen nor have ears heard what God has planned for you, my babies. Continue to make yourselves proud first and then your parents. Love you

To my foster parents: Clarence and Dorothy Lowe, thank you for the years you gave me and making feel special and how you are still in my life today. I love you

To my Godmother, Grace Godwin, you were the place holder I needed that God put in my life. I will forever be grateful of your support, love and dedication to me and my family.

To Bishop Troy V. Carter, you encouraged me to use my wings to fly, you believed in me as a pastor and friend.

To my sister friends: Pastor Betty Spencer, you are such a breath of fresh air thank you for your help, support and love throughout this chapter of my life. You were my midwife when I needed to push.

Pastor Shawna Smith, your prayers and laughter has gotten me through the midnight hour. Just knowing you are there for me has given me the boost I needed to finish this project.

Laveda Lovey Whitfield, I cannot say enough about you. When you look up the word friend in the dictionary, your face is there. We have cried, laughed and became as close as sisters. You have made me do the work. I have found my silent, muted, unused voice, and have started businesses and wrote this book because you allowed God to use you.

Marie Little, Evelyn "Pinky" Blackwell, you've seen me in my weakest moments and never wavered in your love and support for me.

I love you all so much. Thank you

About the Author

Lady Rhonda Brown-Tunstall is a woman of God, the First Lady of New Creation Apostolic Church, Owner of It Takes 2 Fashion Boutique, and CEO of Sowing Seeds of Destiny. Lady Tunstall is a Board-Certified Professional Coach. Her life is dedicated to living by example and encouraging women and teens to live up to their fullest potential. Lady Tunstall has over a decade of experience in the Prince Georges County Board of Education System which enables her to reach others with warmth, humor, transparency and strength. She is a wife, mother, mentor and role-model. Lady Tunstall has been happily married for 26 years to Pastor James William Tunstall. They are the proud parents of D'Andre, Destinee, De'Ja and James.

Author's Note: I would like to thank all of my family and friends, especially those who have supported me and journeyed through this with me. Although my accounts described in this book may differ from others interpretations, this book has been written to help me heal in my journey, Silent Tears No More. It is my prayer that this book be used as a tool for all who read it. He heals the brokenhearted and binds up their wounds. (Psalms 147:3 NIV)

Thanks for reading!

Please add a short review on Amazon and let me know what you thought!

Social Media Sites:

#STNM
Instagram _beautifullymadee
Facebook – Lady Rhonda Brown-Tunstall
Twitter - @allthat4christ

Made in the USA
Middletown, DE
30 May 2019